A–Z
OF
WOKING

PLACES - PEOPLE - HISTORY

Marion Field

AMBERLEY

Acknowledgements

Many thanks to Colin and Ruth Ray, Martin Keys, Kelvin Kingsley, David Staunton-Lambert and Julia Spinks.

First published 2020

Amberley Publishing
The Hill, Stroud, Gloucestershire, GL5 4EP
www.amberley-books.com

Copyright © Marion Field, 2020

The right of Marion Field to be identified as the Author of this work has been asserted in accordance with the Copyrights, Designs and Patents Act 1988.

ISBN 978 1 4456 9310 1 (print)
ISBN 978 1 4456 9311 8 (ebook)

British Library Cataloguing in Publication Data.
A catalogue record for this book is available from the British Library.

Typesetting by Aura Technology and Software Services, India. Printed in Great Britain.

Contents

Introduction

Woking is a rather strange place as its beginnings arose from the building of the railway, which went directly through it. When there was a cholera epidemic in London, all the graveyards were closed. Consequently, it was necessary to find a suitable venue for a new cemetery. What better place than Woking with its new railway? The Member of Parliament at the time was not happy as he said that the Necropolis Company would buy a lot of land, use a small section for the cemetery and sell the rest at a profit. He was proved correct.

The company bought 2,000 acres, but used only 400 for the cemetery. The intention was that Woking would develop on the southern side of the railway; however, the landlord refused to sell the land for development, so the town grew up on the northern side.

The population increased and it became a popular spot for those who worked in the city; however, by the 1990s many were now travelling to work in Woking. The town has seen many changes, and these are still happening in the twenty-first century.

All Saints' Church, Woodham

In 1983 the foundation stone of All Saints' Church in Woodham Lane was laid. By 1894 the church was partially completed. It became a parish in its own right in 1902, but it was not finally completed until 1907. In the twenty-first century it continues to serve the local community as the parish church. Later, a daughter church – St Michael's – was built in Sheerwater. For a while this shared its premises with the Methodist church as there was no Methodist church in the area.

All Saints' Church, Woodham.

Sign at
All Saints'
Church,
Woodham.

Ambassadors Complex

It was not until the 1970s that Woking had its first purpose-built theatre. The Rhoda McGaw Theatre was named after a local councillor who had died in 1971. It seated 230 people. During the latter part of the twentieth century the impressive Ambassadors Complex was built. The small Rhoda McGaw Theatre remained at the bottom of the complex and continues to be used regularly by amateur dramatic groups and operatic societies. Above this is the new Victoria Theatre, which seats 2,000, and there are also six cinema screens.

Ambassadors Complex.

(St) Andrew's School

Church Hill House was built in 1883 by John Buch, the vicar of St Mary the Virgin Church; however, he never lived in it, and over the years it has had several uses. In 1937 St Anne's School had been founded in Mount Hermon Road. In 1947 the school relocated to Church Hill House and was renamed St Andrew's. In 1987 it became a charitable trust.

The 11 acres of surrounding land provide ample space for football and hockey pitches, tennis courts, cricket nets, an indoor swimming pool and an athletics track. As well as regular PE and games lessons, there are various clubs, and matches are played against neighbouring schools.

The balanced curriculum, comprising up-to-date technology, art and design, classics, drama and music, fits pupils for the twenty-first century. Concerts and plays are performed every year and pupils' art is displayed around the building.

The impressive magazine, produced every year, contains photographs, artwork, creative writing and accounts of matches and trips. This fascinating read does great credit to an excellent school.

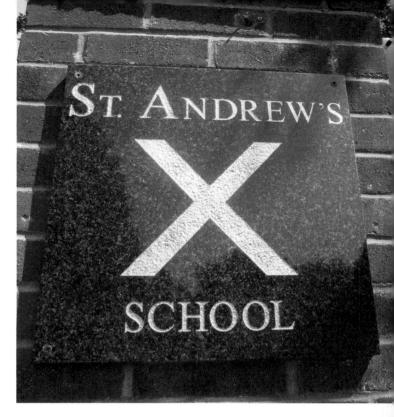

Right: Sign for
St Andrew's School.

Below: St Andrew's School.

Auntie Anne's

Legend suggests that pretzels were invented by an Italian monk in the seventh century. These consisted of overlapping strips of dough, folded to represent praying hands. He called them 'pretiola', which means 'little rewards', and gave them to small children if they had learnt their prayers. Later the name changed to 'brezels' when they were introduced into Germany, and on Easter morning children would go on a 'brezel hunt'. These sweet treats became increasingly popular and in the eighteenth and nineteenth centuries, German immigrants took 'pretzels' to North America.

Anne Beiler was born in Pennsylvania in 1949. As she grew up, she enjoyed baking and making bread and, when she was old enough, she worked on a food stall at a local famers' market. It was here that she learnt to make pretzels in the Pennsylvanian-Dutch style. She progressed to selling her own hand-rolled pretzels at a market stall in Maryland.

Beiler adapted the original recipe to create her own distinctive brand, calling them Auntie Anne's Pretzels. Her first store was opened in a shopping mall near her home, but by 1989 Auntie Anne's Pretzels were found throughout Pennsylvania. Her fame spread and soon there were shops all over the United States and also in Europe. As a devout Christian, she retained the original pattern of praying hands, but felt that they were more like angels' wings so she placed a halo above them for her logo.

In June 2015 Auntie Anne's Pretzels opened in the Peacocks Centre in Woking. Here, customers can enjoy pretzels that come with a 'thirty-minute freshness guarantee'. Coffee is served at a table that has wireless charging stations and power sockets. Both coffee and pretzels can also be taken out. A waitress can often be seen outside the café offering passers-by small pretzel samples to try.

Auntie Anne's Pretzel Bakery.

B

(The) Bedser Twins

Eric and Alec Bedser, the famous twins, were six months old when their father moved his family to Woking, where they lived for the rest of their lives. The twins were educated at Maybury Junior School and Monument Hill Secondary School, and the family attended All Saints' Church in Woodham where the twins sang in the choir.

They were seven when they played their first cricket match and at age fourteen they became members of Woking Cricket Club. Their talent was soon recognised and, in 1938, they joined the staff at Surrey Cricket Ground, the Oval. The following year they played their first match for Surrey against Oxford University.

Below left: Alec Bedser.

Below right: Eric Bedser.

Their cricketing careers were put on hold during the war when they served in the RAF. They resumed playing after the cessation of hostilities and both continued to play for Surrey. In 1946 Alec played in his first Test match against India, and, in the same year, he joined the England team on the Australian tour. Both twins continued to play for Surrey, but Alec also represented England. He played his last Test match in July 1955 against South Africa.

Both twins retired from professional cricket in 1960. Alec became president of the Surrey Cricket Club. In 1965 he received in OBE, and a CBE in 1982. Then in 1997 he was knighted by the Queen for his services to cricket. Eric died in 2006 and Alec followed him four years later in 2010.

(The) Big Apple

The Big Apple appeared at the end of the twentieth century. Situated in Commercial Road, it is described as the 'top local venue for a wide range of exciting entertainment'. It caters for all ages and has easy access for wheelchairs. The ten-pin bowling area contains all the latest equipment, including lane bumpers and ball ramps. Children's birthdays can be celebrated by bowling parties.

The Big Apple.

Laserquest is situated in a large multi-level, maze-like arena containing ramps and catwalks. Here, visitors can enjoy a laser tag team game, shooting opponents with laser guns. Another area, Planet Zoom, provides 'fun and magic for kids'. This contains snake slides, fun activity towers and colourful ball parks. There is, of course, a café where visitors can sample a cup of coffee and a variety of refreshments.

Bird in Hand

The Bird in Hand in Mayford has always been owned by individuals. At one time the owner was a Mr Enzo, who also owned Engo's Wine Bar. The extension he built onto the original building is now the restaurant, which is separate from the bar area. Later owners failed to keep the pub in a state of good repair, and by the twenty-first century it needed a great deal of restoration and its popularity had declined.

Bird in Hand.

Markus Hebbourne and Mike Cumberland were two local young men who had worked in other pubs in the area. They decided to take over the Bird in Hand and restore it to its former glory. They carried out extensive renovations and by October 2015 it was again open for business.

Comfortable sofas and intimate areas were provided in the bar area, while the spacious dining room was lit by skylights and Edison lamps. Potted plants provided splashes of colour, and on the walls were paintings of bygone days. The extensive experimental menu lacked some of the traditional staple dishes but provided a variety of other tempting delights. Sandwiches and wraps were available at lunchtime and the traditional Sunday roast is, of course, served every week.

The dessert menu is experimental, and the traditional banana split is caramelised and served with a mille-feuille wafer. Evening events include a tapas night, a steak and cheese night and wine tastings. The Bird in Hand is well worth a visit.

Brewery Road

At one time a brewery functioned in Horsell. Today the only reminders of it are the names of roads Brewery Road and Old Malt Way.

Brewery Road.

Bridge Barn

On the banks of the Basingstoke Canal stands Bridge Barn – now a Beefeater restaurant. It is likely that the building was originally built in the sixteenth century, and some parts of the old building still remain. Built as a farm building, as the name suggests, by the nineteenth century it had fallen into disuse. The land surrounding it was then used as a nursery.

During this time the area around Bridge Barn was developed and new roads were built. Part of the original building had become a cottage and, in the mid-twentieth century, the nursery gave way to a riding school, which flourished on the site until more roads and increased traffic forced it to close.

Bridge Barn became a restaurant situated in a cul-de-sac – Bridge Barn Lane. The restaurant has changed hands several times since its inception, but today it is a Beefeater restaurant. Open all day, it serves a cooked or Continental breakfast and a variety of dishes for lunch and dinner. There are tables in the garden beside the canal and when the weather is suitable visitors can enjoy a drink or a meal beside the water.

Inside, there are tables in the bar area, while the restaurant on the upper floor is on two levels. Many of the seats overlook the canal. Bridge Barn is a popular venue at all times of the day; however, it is always full at Sunday lunchtimes when a selection of three delicious roasts are on offer.

Bridge Barn.

Bridge Barn.

Brynford Close

St Michael's School was originally housed in the building that is now the Shaw Centre. When it needed a larger building the school moved to Brynford, at the corner of Grange Road and Woodham Road. Sadly, the house has now been demolished but the name lives on with the road that passed through the new houses – Brynford Close.

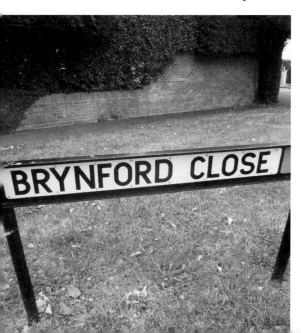

Brynford Close.

C

Canal

The Wey Navigation development started in the late seventeenth century when the area near the River Wey was improved. The population increased in the nearby villages of St John's and Knaphill. In 1787 the building of the Basingstoke Canal was authorised by Parliament, and ten years later work started on the canal at Woodham. Bricks from the local brickworks were used for the building of the bridges and locks. It was not until 1913 that Wheatsheaf Bridge, built of local bricks, was replaced with a metal bridge.

In September 1795 the Basingstoke Canal was completed and proved extremely useful for transporting timber, coal and other materials. The canal continued to be used until the mid-nineteenth century when the railway was built. Having transported materials for the laying of the railway line, the canal was no longer needed for transport and fell into disrepair.

In 1966 the Surry and Hampshire Canal Society was formed, and in 1977 restoration work started on the canal. In 1991 it was finally reopened for leisure use. Identified now

The canal.

Canal Festival.

as a Site of Special Scientific Interest, it contains the largest variety of aquatic plants and invertebrates in the United Kingdom. Woking Canal Festival was held in August 2016 to celebrate twenty-five years since its reopening. Also celebrated at the same time was the fiftieth anniversary of the founding of the Surrey and Hampshire Canal Society.

Until fairly recently, a canal festival was held annually at Easter when decorated barges made their stately way along the canal. Today, in the summer, visitors can enjoy the popular canal trips on specially adapted barges.

(The) Cardinals

Woking Football Club was founded in 1889. Known as the Woking Cardinals, their home ground is in Kingfield Stadium, next to the David Lloyd Centre. Both players and fans have always had a reputation for fair play and good behaviour.

In January 1991, Woking beat West Bromwich Albion 4-2 in the third round FA Cup tie. The match was played in the latter's ground. The hero of the game was Woking's Tim Buzaglo, who scored three goals in fifteen minutes. His opponents were so impressed that that, after the match, they hoisted him aloft and paraded him around the ground to cheers from both sides. His fifteen minutes of fame even attracted the attention of the national press.

In the fourth round the Cardinals lost to Everton, but they played so well that they were given a standing ovation by the crowd and were described by the Everton manager as a 'fine team'. The year 1994 was a memorable one for the Cardinals. In May of that year thousands of fans sporting red and white caps and scarves and waving red and white flags descended on Wembley Stadium to watch their team defeat Runcom in the FA Trophy final. The fans were euphoric as they boarded the train at Waterloo; it was a very good-natured crowd. Woking celebrated the team's victory the following week with a victory parade around the town, ending with a civic reception at Woking Leisure Centre.

The Cardinals have played well, and successfully, throughout the twentieth and twenty-first centuries and they continue to be supported by their vast arm of well-behaved fans.

Chapel Corner

In 1815 a small Baptist chapel was built in Horsell Common on the front of two existing cottages. The trustees signed the trust deed on vellum. Because some of them were illiterate, they signed only with a cross. Beside the chapel there was room for a small graveyard. The congregation flourished, but over the years the building deteriorated. It was not until 1907 that the building was renovated. In 1935 the oil lamps were replaced by electricity. Over the following years the congregation declined and there were no newcomers.

In 1963, Mr Sydney Fleet, a member of a local Brethren group, bought the chapel and it became a place of worship for the Brethren. Mr and Mrs Fleet lived in the cottages behind the chapel. Mr Fleet died in 1986 and the chapel was no longer used for worship.

Chapel Corner.

Andrew Fleet, his son, eventually demolished the deteriorating building. He obtained permission from the Home Office to remove the gravestones from the graveyard, but the bodies remained. On the site Andrew built a house and the graveyard became an attractive garden. The new house was appropriately named Chapel Corner and Andrew and his wife Valerie continue to live in it. A stained-glass window featuring the original chapel was inserted into the front door of Chapel Corner as a reminder that the site had once been a place of worship.

Christ Church

In the 1970s there was no church in the centre of Woking and services were held in a room above a shop in Chertsey Road. When the congregation outgrew it, an iron room was built on the empty site destined for a new church in the centre of the town. It was not until 1887 that enough money had been found to start building. The Duchess of Albany, a daughter-in-law of Queen Victoria, laid the foundation stone.

Building was finally completed in 1893. At the time Woking lay in the diocese of Winchester, and the bishop led the consecration service on 14 June. The diocese

Christ Church.

decided that Christ Church should become a parish in its own right, and on 29 August 1893 William Hamilton was installed as the first vicar.

During the twentieth century the building was adapted to accommodate the growing congregation. Several rooms above the church continue to be used for church activity, as well as being available for community groups. During the Christmas period one of the rooms is used as a Christmas charity card shop. At the millennium the pews were replaced by chairs and the west end of the church became a popular coffee shop, serving breakfasts and light lunches. Next to the coffee shop, on the north side, is the Origin Bookshop, stocking a variety of books and also cards and gifts.

Church of the Good Shepherd

The population of Pyrford, near Woking, expanded during the twentieth century and a new church was needed. In 1936 a site for this was purchased but the Second World War hindered its building. Construction finally started in 1962 and it took two years to build. When completed, the church could seat 600. In 1964 the Church of the Good Shepherd was consecrated and continued to increase in numbers during the rest of the twentieth century. To celebrate the millennium an extra chapel was added.

Church of the
Good Shepherd.

The population continued to grow and in 2005 the building was enlarged to provide extra room and a larger hall. The facilities are used throughout the week by both the congregation and the wider community. Services continue to be held regularly on Sundays and occasionally there is a four o' clock family service, followed by tea and cake. A variety of activities cater for both young and old. There are women's breakfasts, men's curry evenings, a youth club and a number of events for children. The church and its facilities are a hive of activity throughout the year.

Church of the Holy Cross

In 1861 Benjamin and Rosamira Lancaster from Kilburn found the Anglican Order of St Peter in order to provide for the 'nursing of ladies in bad health and narrow circumstances'. When, in 1883, the order was given land in Woking for 'use as they saw fit', Benjamin provided money to build the Home for Incurables. The foundation stone was laid and building was completed two years later. It opened in 1885 with forty nuns caring for sixty patients.

In 1898 the foundation stone for a chapel was laid near the home. It was designed by the famous architect John Loughborough Parson and was considered to be his finest work. It was dedicated to St Peter, and on the south wall a brass plate can be seen that commemorating the order's founder, Benjamin Lancaster. Another commemorative brass plate remembers Revd W. H. Cleaver, the first warden of the community; he served for forty-four years. In 1900 an organ was installed and in 1984 the chapel became a Grade I listed building. An interesting feature at the top of the steps leading to the crypt is a hand-operated lift used to carry wheelchair patients.

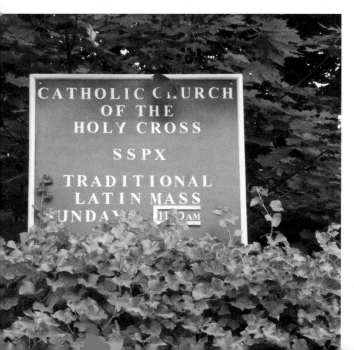

The Holy Cross.

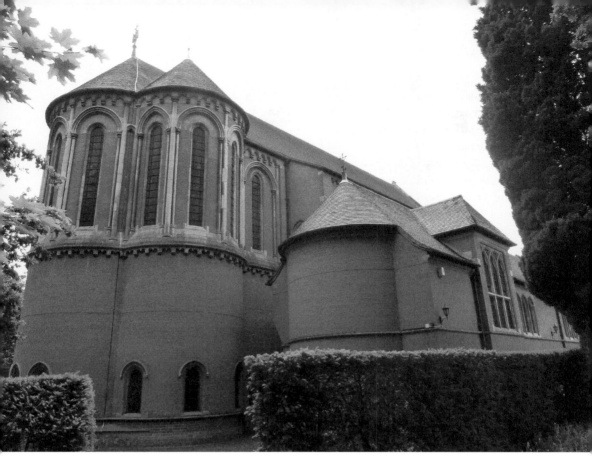

Church of the Holy Cross.

Over the years the nuns became fewer and in 1996 the Roman Catholic Society of St Pius X took over the chapel and renamed it the Church of the Holy Cross. A new altar and a baptismal font were installed, and statues of saints appeared around the chapel. Today it has a loyal congregation who regularly attend Mass.

In 2004, the home, which had become St Peter's Convent, closed and was converted into a luxurious apartment building.

Courtney Free Church

The Courtney Free Church, situated at the end of Walton Road, had its origins at the beginning of the twentieth century in Courtney Road at the other end of Woking. A number of people felt the need for a place of worship in the area. A hall, which had originally been used as a laundry, was adapted for worship for the congregation of thirty. The group became known as the Courtney Road Fellowship, but by 1908 it had outgrown its premises.

A nearby builder's workshop had recently become vacant, so the ground floor was taken over by the fellowship and adapted to accommodate its congregation, which

Courtney Free Church.

had by now grown to 140. This continued to be used until 1922 when the lease ran out and the building was sold.

The fellowship had attracted the attention of a wealthy businessman who gifted some land in Courtney Road to them. He also paid £600 for a new building for worship to be erected. This was done within two months and a service of dedication was held on 4 October 1922. Extra rooms were later added and these premises were used for forty years. In 1944 the group changed its name to Courtney Free Church.

Unfortunately, in the 1960s the area was scheduled for redevelopment by Woking Borough Council and once more the group had to look for another home. At the end of Walton Road a Mission Hall had been built in 1906 to be used by St Paul's Church in Oriental Road. When, in the 1960s, a new church hall was built on to the existing church, the Mission Hall was no longer needed. It was an ideal site for Courtney Free Church, which took it over in 1967.

The hall was renovated and a heated pool for baptism was installed. Services are regularly held and local groups are able to use the hall for meetings.

Crematorium

In 1878 Sir Henry Thompson, Queen Victoria's physician and president of the Cremation Society of Great Britain, bought an area of land near St John's village. Professor Paolo Gorini from Italy was commissioned to conduct a freestanding cremator. The first custom-built crematorium in the United Kingdom was built on the site. Cremation was still illegal in England at this time, but the apparatus was tested successfully by using the carcase of a horse.

In 1884 an Act legalising cremation was passed by Parliament, and the first human cremation in Woking took place on 26 March 1885. There was still a great deal of hostility, but cremation gradually became popular and, by the end of the nineteenth century, nearly 2,000 cremations had taken place.

A chapel containing a new crematorium was erected in 1888 when waiting rooms and other amenities were also added. When more land was acquired at a later date, the Garden of Remembrance was created.

The Crematorium.

David Lloyd Leisure Centre

In 1985 Chris Lane opened his leisure centre in Westfield Avenue. A plastic dome covered the four indoor tennis courts and there was a small club room nearby. The club flourished and acquired a reputation for excellence. By the twenty-first century there were nearly 5,000 adult members and over 1,000 juniors.

David Lloyd Centre.

Additions to the club included four more indoor tennis courts, four outdoor tennis courts, a gym and a health and beauty spa. Chris Lane had built up his excellent leisure centre and he felt ready to pass it on. In 2002 he sold it to Whitbread who were responsible for the David Lloyd leisure centres. The name was changed to the David Lloyd Leisure Centre, and its reputation for excellence continued.

Tennis competitions were introduced; matches against other clubs were enjoyed by the men's team, the ladies' team and the mixed team. There were also 'Club Sessions' for those who preferred to play socially. The gym continued to be popular and in addition to the new indoor swimming pool a sauna and a steam room were also introduced. The health and beauty spa was replaced with a physiotherapy room; a variety of activities for both young and old take place in a spacious studio, and a crèche is provided. The welcoming café provides, as expected, a 'Balanced choice of meals and snacks to complement a healthy lifestyle'.

Davison, Peter

Soon after he was born in 1951, Peter Moffett's family moved to Knaphill. When he reached secondary school age, Peter attended Winston Churchill School. While there, his acting talent blossomed, and he became a member of the Byfleet Players. Occasionally, in his spare time, he pulled pints at his local pub, the Wheatsheaf, in Chobham Road.

He later studied at the Central School of Speech and Drama. His first job after leaving was as assistant manager at the Nottingham Playhouse. Because another actor had the name of Moffatt, Peter changed his name to Davison. During the 1970s he appeared on television several times, but his break came in 1978 when he was cast as Tristan Farnon in *All Creatures Great and Small*. The real Tristan Farnon helped him to create his role. It was in 1980 that he signed a contract to succeed Tom Baker as the iconic Doctor in *Doctor Who*. His first series aired in 1982. He was the youngest actor at the time to have played the role, and he continued in it until 1984. In 1988 Peter was persuaded to play Tristan Farnon again in a revival of *All Creatures Great and Small*. He is rarely out of work and continues to appear in television, films and on stage as well as on the radio. In 1982 Eamonn Andrews hosted Peter Davison's appearance on the television show *This is Your Life*.

(St) Dunstan's Church

In 1899 an iron church was built in Percy Street for the use of the Roman Catholics. Dedicated to St Dunstan, it was used until the 1920s. When Father Plummer became the new parish priest in 1923 he decided that a new building was necessary. The foundation stone on an empty site in Heathside Crescent was laid and building commenced. Two years later the new St Dunstan's Church was completed and the first Mass was held in December 1925. Father Plummer died in 1954 and he was buried in the grounds beside the church.

As the Catholic population grew, two other churches were built in Woking. When, after the Second World War, many Italians settled in Woking, Masses were held in Italian as well as English. At the beginning of the twenty-first century Heathside Crescent was scheduled for redevelopment and St Dunstan's had to find a new home. This was at the corner of Shaftesbury Road and Pembroke Road – the site had originally housed St Francis School.

In 2006 work started on the new church and it was dedicated in October of that year by the Bishop of Arundel and Brighton. The remains of Father Plummer were reinterred in a cemetery near St Edward the Confessor Chapel in Sutton Green. The church continues to serve a large congregation, and the large hall that adjoins it is in regular use by the community as well as the congregation. During Lent, 'Lent Lunches', supported by other churches in the area, are held in the hall.

St Dunstan's Church.

E

Elia

Elia, situated in Commercial Way, first opened its doors in November 2018. It is an independent Greek restaurant run by a husband and wife team, Antela and Peter Elizaj, and their son Joel. The name 'Elia' is Greek for olive and the Greek theme is used in the decoration of the restaurant. The ceiling shows the brown leaves of an olive tree painted by local artist Laura Carrillo. Her paintings, which are for sale, hang on the walls.

The menu is mainly Greek, prepared by a Greek chef and influenced by Antela's Greek grandmother's recipes. The meat served is provided by local Surrey butchers and is organic. The meze is a delight, consisting of a selection of traditional Greek dishes – taramasalata, chickpeas olives, feta cheese, pitta bread and humous. Other Mediterranean dishes are also on offer.

The restaurant is closed on Mondays but is open from 11 a.m. to 11 p.m. from Tuesday to Saturday. On Sundays it opens at 11 a.m. as usual but closes at 6 p.m. Since its opening, Elia has become a popular meeting place for lunch and dinner and has attracted some excellent reviews from diners. Its attractive dining area has the relaxed atmosphere of a traditional Greek taverna, and Antela and Peter are happy to host private parties.

Meze platter at Elia's restaurant.

Floods

At certain times floods have plagued Woking and the surrounding area. The twentieth century started off with the worst floods for over forty years. In some houses the occupants had to camp upstairs as the water was several feet deep. Old Woking had become a lake. A nearby brewery was flooded and beer barrels floated down the High Street, so Old Woking's residents acquired a floating public house. The water also attracted a gaggle of geese who amused themselves by swimming in one window of a house and out through another one.

In what had been a field, a young horse, which had been happily grazing, was submerged in water up to its knees. The enterprising farmer used a boat to rescue the terrified animal. Unfortunately, the horse was not very cooperative and the boat almost capsized; however, eventually they reached some unflooded land and the horse appeared the worse for its experience.

Twenty years later and floods struck again; Old Woking once more resembled a lake. This time it was swans who enjoyed the unexpected water. They sailed gracefully up and down the High Street followed by their brood of cygnets. Residents, marooned upstairs in their houses, threw bread out of the windows to the beautiful creatures. These offerings were graciously received.

A human resident showed great enterprise by carrying two chairs with him to aid his long journey to dry land. There have been other floods over the years and no doubt there will be more in the future.

Food and Drink Festival

Woking's Food and Drink Festival was held first in 2013. Since then, it has been held annually at the beginning of September and each year has become more ambitious. The free festival takes place in the town centre and for three days visitors can sample a variety of delicious dishes, enjoy some entertainment and take part in activities.

The Woking Shopping Demo Theatre in Jubilee Square is where both celebrity and local chefs provide twenty cookery demonstrations for the visitors. Other pedestrian

Woking Food Festival.

areas are occupied by eighty food and drink stalls, stocked with artisan products and freshly cooked dishes from around the United Kingdom and across the world.

Wine masterclasses and tastings are also on offer. Something new was offered in 2019: a pop-up dining experience taking place at various venues around the town. Among other delights was a curry supper, a jazz brunch, and an afternoon tea.

Also on offer were bite-sized talks on a variety of subjects including English wine, beekeeping, spices, brewing and gin distilling. All could also enjoy the humorous street entertainers and the live music provided. Children were not forgotten either; there were art and craft workshops including cupcake decorating. The Woking Food and Drink Festival will definitely be taking place for many years to come.

Fuel Cell

In the 1940s Sir William Grove, a professor of physics at the London Institute, developed the idea of a fuel cell. Over 150 years later Woking utilised his idea, becoming the first borough in the country to be powered by a fuel cell. Hydrogen and oxygen were fed into the cell to produce electricity and water.

In 2003 a newly landscaped garden in Woking Park became the site for the new Woking fuel cell. The garden was irrigated by water from the cell. Named Grove Garden in honour of Sir William, a statue of the physicist was erected nearby. Richard Sanderson, Mayor of Woking, performed the opening ceremony and unveiled the statue in front of a number of VIPs, including some descendants of Sir William.

Greenfield School

Situated at the end of Constitution Hill, in 1922 Denham House became a dame school. It changed hands in the 1930s and became Greenfield School. In 1948 Ruth Hicks bought nearby Beechlands. She and Joyce Pearce took over Greenfield School and the school moved to its new premises. Ruth Hicks became the headmistress and it continued to use the building in Constitution Hill until September 2019 when Greenfield School moved its premises to the corner of East Hill and the Old Woking Road. This was the original site of the new Girls' Grammar School and later this had been replaced by the International School.

The original Greenfield School.

Gordon's School

Charles George Gordon was killed in Khartoun on 26 January 1855. Gordon Boys' School in West End was founded in his memory in the late nineteenth century. Its pupils were the sons of those who had served in the British Army. The school received its first colour in 1895 and this was laid on the altar at the start of every Sunday morning service.

In July 1955 a new colour was presented to the school by the Duke of Edinburgh. Dressed in his uniform of field marshal, he was escorted to the dais outside the building by the chairman of the governors, Viscount Cunningham, who was Admiral of the Fleet. It was an impressive occasion with many VIPs present. The old colour was paraded around the grounds before being carried into the school; the doors closed behind it.

After receiving the new colour from Major Edwards of the Cadet Corps, the duke presented it to Sergeant Turnball. The ceremony 'Trooping the Colour' followed. During the following service, the Bishop of Guildford consecrated the new colour and the school prayer concluded the service.

In the school grounds stands a statue of General Gordon seated on a camel. This was designed in 1902 by Onslow Ford. It was erected in London and remained there until 1904 when it was sent to Khartoun. In January 1959 a new regime in Sudan decided that the statue should be returned to England. It was hauled on board the troopship *Fort Dunvegan* and began the long sea voyage to England where it arrived in April. The Foreign Office had decided that it should be erected in the grounds of Gordon Boys' School. Loaded onto a lorry for the journey, it was eventually erected on an appropriate site.

In September 1990 girls were admitted to the school for the first time and the name was changed to Gordon's School.

Gypsies in Woking

Gypsy communities have travelled in Britain for at least 500 years and have camped in Surrey since the sixteenth century. However, there was sometimes friction between the travelling gypsies and families who lived in houses. Henry VIII did not tolerate them and during his reign anyone known to be a gypsy could be executed.

In 1905 George Rastrick, a Woking landowner, allowed gypsies to camp on his land; however, because of this he came into conflict with Woking Urban District Council, who considered that the encampment had 'become a nuisance dangerous to health'. The council demanded that he remove the gypsies from his land. When he refused, he was taken to court. He was a solicitor by profession, so he defended his tenants in court himself, but lost the case. The gypsies were ordered off his land and travelled to find a more hospitable home.

There was another gypsy settlement near Kingfield, and the vicar of St Peter's Church often visited them. He even persuaded them to legalise their unions by having marriage services in St Peter's Church. He must have been very persuasive, as in December 1906 there were ten gypsy weddings on ten consecutive days in the church. They varied in age from twenty to fifty-five and included two generations of one family. The ceremonies were free of charge and the vicar provided the witnesses.

Another encampment of around ninety gypsies living in tents and caravans occupied a site in Well Lane, Horsell. They paid rent to Earnest Lambert, a carpenter, who owned the land. Chertsey Rural District Council, which was responsible for the area, was not happy with the situation. In 1907 Lambert ignored the council's instructions to 'abate the nuisance' on his land. The area was a health hazard because of the state of the soggy filthy ground. Human and animal waste from the closets and nearby cesspits had flowed into the slough of mud. Lambert was taken to court and fined. The council then took charge of the area, cleaning it and reducing the number of gypsies who could live there. They continued there until the middle of the twentieth century.

Born and bred on the land, gypsies lived in caravans that were drawn by horses, and tents. The horses, attached by rope to a long pole, grazed on the land. During the day the children would usually go to the local schools. The men would sometimes go away to work, but always returned to the camp in the summer. They resisted repeated attempts to persuade them to live in houses. 'We don't know bricks and mortar. Caravans are all we know'. Some, but not all, of the villagers were happy to provide them with buckets of water when needed.

They visited the local houses, persuading the housewives to buy their goods, which were anything that they had found to sell – pegs and props for washing lines were popular. Some houseowners would provide them with items that they could sell. In the evening fires were lit to cook their meal, which would be eaten outside. Afterwards stories would be told until bedtime.

The latter part of the twentieth century saw a rise in reaction against the gypsies, and in 1960 an Act was passed giving local councils the power to remove them from their campsites and relocate them in houses. The gypsies were not happy and found it hard to adjust. The women would sit on the kerb outside their houses garbed in colourful shawls with their bare feet on the road while breastfeeding their babies.

Eventually realising that gypsies needed their own space, another Act was passed in 1968. This instructed local councils that they must provide caravan sites throughout the country to provide for them. Today most local people are more tolerant, but occasionally there is friction and the travellers have to be moved on to another site.

Heater's Bakery

Bread has been England's staple diet for many years, but it was not until 1869 that a bakery opened in Church Path in Woking. Freshly baked bread and delicious cakes could be bought from the Health Bakery. In 1943 the bakery was taken over by Frederick Heater, who opened more shops under his name Heater's. Today the company is still run by the Heater family. Heater's the Baker and Sandwich Maker situated in Guildford Road serves a wide selection of sandwiches, Danish pastries, cakes and other freshly baked delights. It is definitely worth a visit.

High Street

The High Street runs beside the railway line, and in the late nineteenth century shops were built there. In 1914 a new gentlemen's outfitters opened. Named after the owner, High Harris, it sold both leisure and more formal attire. It also boasted a vast array of

High Street mural.

hats, which were displayed in one of the windows. Unlike today, no gentleman would be seen outside his house without the appropriate hat on his head. There were caps and hats to suit every occasion.

Hugh Harris retired in 1946 and sold his shop to Henry Martin. His son Paul took it over when his father retired. In the 1990s Paul Martin persuaded Woking Borough Council to erect a mural on the railway embankment. This was to illustrate the various shops that had served customers in the High Street from the nineteenth century to the first half of the twentieth century. Hugh Harris was, of course, included and Lee Simpson, the current manager of the shop, could be seen at his desk.

Sadly, High Harris has now closed, and by the twenty-first century most of the shops had changed hands many times; however, the High street remains busy and the mural can still be enjoyed by shoppers.

Hoe Place

In 1620, James I granted the manor of Woking to Sir Edward Zouch. By now the palace needed a great deal of repair, but Sir Edward was not interested in repairing it. Instead, he removed a number of bricks from its decaying walls and used them to build himself a luxurious manor house nearby. Here, he enjoyed entertaining. One of his frequent visitors was Lady Castlemaine, a mistress of Charles II. She used it as a retreat from her busy social life in London.

The house was later sold to the Booth family, in whose hands it remained until the 1920s. In 1928 it was taken over by Hoe Place Preparatory School. This became merged with St Michael's School in 1964. Then in 1986 it merged with Allen House, a Guildford school, to became Hoe Bridge School – a name it still bears.

Today it is an independent school catering for girls and boys between the ages of three and thirteen. Set in 22 acres of beautiful parkland on the outskirts of Woking, it has an excellent reputation. In 2012 plans were approved for the development of a new performing arts centre and an extension to the dining room. Currently the small dining room holds three lunch sittings for its 340 pupils and forty staff, so the lunch period is

Hoe Bridge School.

rather rushed. The new spacious venue with its flexible 'caterpillar' tables would enable pupils and staff to eat together at the same time in a more relaxed atmosphere.

The new performing arts centre will contain a multipurpose rehearsal auditorium where concerts, plays and dance performances can be held. The new lecture hall will be an excellent venue for visiting speakers. The new complex will also be able to host outside events and workshops as well as providing extra indoor space for the popular holiday camps. It was opened in 2019.

Hollywood House

On 12 April 1930 Woking's third cinema was officially opened in Chobham Road by Mr Godfrey Nicholson, the MP for Farnham. Described as 'one of the finest cinemas in the UK', it was named The Ritz. A specially built Compton organ was installed. New modern projection technology was used, and audiences enjoyed the comfort of air conditioning in the hot weather and central heating in the cold.

There was a restaurant on the floor above the cinema and during matinee performances spectators could have afternoon tea brought to them in their seats. As the restaurant was open all day, it was used by others as well as cinemagoers.

Hollywood House.

Sadly, the cinema closed during the latter part of the twentieth century and for some time the building was used as a bingo hall. In 1988 the building was demolished and replaced by an office block, appropriately named Hollywood House – the only reminder of the 'silver screen'.

Horsell Parish Hall

In 1923 a number of thespians in Horsell performed a play, *Our Flat*, to an invited audience. It was a great success and more productions were requested. This led to the formation of Horsell Amateur Dramatic Society (HADS).

Its first production was a comedy, *The Man from Toronto* by Douglas Murray. The performance took place in Horsell Parish Hall on 2 February 1922 in front of an audience wearing evening dress. Its success inspired more thespians to join the society; one of these was Patrick Moore, who was teaching at the nearby St Andrew's Preparatory School.

The society flourished and many more performances were seen on the stage of the Parish Hall. When in the 1970s a new purpose-built theatre was opened in Woking for the first time, HADS transferred its performances to the Rhoda McGaw Theatre, which was named after a local councillor.

Today, in the twenty-first century, the society continues to hold auditions and rehearsals in the Parish Hall. Other groups have also used the hall over the years for meetings, parties and celebrations. It will no doubt continue to be a vital part of the village for many years to come.

Stage door at Horsell Parish Hall.

I

Inkerman Road

On 22 May 1860 a prison housing 300 male and female inmates was officially opened in Knaphill. A second building to house the female prisoners was built in 1867. This was officially opened in 1869, by which time it held seventy women.

In 1889 the male prison closed and the Royal Engineers took possession of it. The building was named Inkerman Barracks, and when the female prison closed in 1899 it became the home of the Royal Artillery. The army continued to use the barracks until 1965 when the area was taken over by Woking Borough Council for redevelopment. Today the only reminder of the army's presence is Inkerman Road.

Jackman's Nursery

In the early nineteenth century William Jackman established his nursery in Goldsworth Road. In 1870 he also acquired the nearby nursery, which had been founded by James Turner in 1760. Jackman's Nursery became the most popular one in the area. It produced a variety of seeds, flowers and shrubs. Later, a café was opened to serve visitors.

Woking Garden Centre.

In the late twentieth century it became part of the Garden Centre Group and took the name Woking Garden Centre. In the twenty-first century it was taken over by Wyevale, which continued to run it until 2019 when it was sold to another company. It has now reverted to its previous name of Woking Garden Centre and continues to produce the wide variety of plants for which it has always been famous. The café is still a popular venue for meeting friends for breakfast, lunch and afternoon tea.

(St) John's Church

Because of the flourishing brickworks at the west end of Woking, the population grew during the nineteenth century. However, there was no church in the area and it was felt that one was needed. A small chapel of ease linked to St Peter's Church was built in 1842 to accommodate the growing population. It was dedicated to St John the Baptist, and the surrounding village became known as St John's. In 1883 it became a parish in its own right. Today it has a flourishing congregation and welcomes other members of the community to participate in a variety of activities throughout the week.

St John's Church.

Kitty

Kitty is a delightful twelve-seater boat, named after the last horse that pulled a barge along the canal. Her inaugural cruise on the Basingstoke Canal was in 2016, and during the first year she attracted 400 visitors; they came not only from the local area, but also from around the world. Since then, *Kitty* has been part of the tourist scene in Woking. She is crewed by qualified volunteers from the Basingstoke Canal Society who have been trained by the Royal Yacht Association.

During the summer, trips are available at weekends, Wednesdays and bank holidays. They run three times a day at 11 a.m., 1 p.m. and 2.45 p.m. During August there are also trips on Fridays. Trips start at the Town Wharf, near the Brewery Road Car Park, and last around one and a quarter hours if there are no stops. Passengers enjoy a peaceful trip gliding along the Basingstoke Canal. They may see herons, kingfishers, duck, moorhens, swans and even turtles.

Individuals as well as families cruise past Horsell Common near where in H. G. Wells' famous novel *War of the Worlds*, Martians landed and proceeded to destroy the town of Woking. Charter trips for special occasions can also be booked for either morning or afternoon and the *Kitty* is suitable for all weathers; she also has wheelchair access. The trip provides a relaxing hour in a busy life as passengers view the town from a different, more peaceful perspective.

Library

In the twentieth century the local council decided that the town needed a public library. Suitable premises were eventually found in a derelict Roman Catholic chapel in Percy Street. This was adapted for its new use, and in 1928 Woking's first public library was open for business. It provided a wide variety of reading matter and Woking residents flocked to borrow books.

It was not long before larger premises were needed. There was a Methodist chapel in Chapel Street and when, in 1934, the Methodists moved to new premises, the

Below left: The original Woking Library.

Below right: Woking Library today.

Café Rouge.

library took over the empty chapel, which was an ideal venue and was able to house an increasing number of books.

In the latter part of the twentieth century, Woking was once again being redeveloped and the library building was due for demolition. For the first time a large purpose-built library was erected in Commercial Road and even more books were added. This was used for only a short time and in 1992 the library was relocated to yet another new building in the town centre opposite the war memorial. Even this was not its final resting place.

On this occasion it was shunted back towards the canal to make room for the prestigious Café Rouge, which opened its doors in 2013. Today, the library boasts computers with updated technology, tables where students can sit and research and armchairs where visitors can relax and brows though the latest newspapers and magazines.

(The) Lightbox

The Lightbox, on the corner of Chobham Road and Victoria Way, opened in September 2007. The following February it was officially opened by the Duke of Kent. The same year it won the Museum of the Year award from the Art Fund. In 2016 it was also awarded a Green Tourist Silver Award.

Every year the box-shaped building holds a number of temporary exhibitions on the upper floors. The permanent exhibition on the lower floor that illustrates Woking's

Lightbox.

history is frequently updated by a number of enthusiastic volunteers. One of these always greets visitors at the entrance and also acts as a guide. The café on the ground floor provides snacks and lunches every day, except on Mondays, when the Lightbox is closed. This is also used on occasion for celebration dinners.

In 2017 the Lightbox hosted Woking's first Literary Festival, and on one evening a dinner was held in the café to celebrate Jane Austen. This was followed by the film *Pride and Prejudice* in one of the rooms on the upper floor. The following year, during the second Literary Festival, the Brontës were celebrated. The Woking Literary Festival is now an annual event. With its talks, workshops, films and poetry readings, it is very popular and is becoming widely known.

Literary Festival

Woking's first Literary Festival was held in the Lightbox in April 2017. It was so successful that it is now an annual event, running for ten days every April. It caters for all ages, including an interactive experience for children. A popular event, usually held on the second Saturday, is the open-mic poetry day when budding and experienced poets can read their work to an appreciative audience.

There are a number of talks by local authors and others including Alison Weir, who is writing books about each of Henry VIII's wives. In 2019 she had just completed the life of the fourth wife, Anne of Cleves, who was lucky to keep her head on her shoulders unlike her predecessor, poor Anne Boleyn.

Also in 2019, a local author, Richard Langtree, spoke about his forthcoming biography of Revd William Hamilton who had been the vicar of Christ Church and generously provided money for the building of St Paul's Church in Maybury. Richard told his audience that he had spent fifteen years researching the life of this interesting man.

In 2019 the festival ended with a workshop for budding authors.

Lion House

James Walker was a trained engineer who realised that effective packing was required to protect the products of an engineering plant. His strong packaging was patented in 1888. 'Lion' was his commercial brand name, and the first Walker Lion trademark for his packaging was used in March 1889.

The company continued to expand and in 1911 James Walker & Co. became a limited company. When James Walker died in 1913, George Cook became chairman. Advertised as 'Lion, the King of Packings', the company soon needed larger buildings. In 1926 the site in Oriental Road, which had once housed the now defunct Martynside Aircraft Factory, was bought.

The Lion Works continued to function on the site for many years; however, in 1993 the site was closed and the buildings were demolished. James Walker & Co. continued to flourish, however, and Lion House, built on the site, is now its headquarters. The Lion Shopping Park now has pride of place beside this – a reminder of its former function.

Above: Lion Retail Park.

Left: Lion House.

M

Maggie G

Margaret Gammon, who died in 2019, was a Conservative councillor for thirty-one years and had been elected Mayor of Woking twice. In 2003 she was awarded an MBE for services to the community and she retired the following year. She had a vision that boat trips should be available for those who, for one reason for another, were not able to travel on the other boats that sailed on the Basingstoke Canal.

To this end she formed a committee, Woking Recreational Boating for the Handicapped, which started to raise funds. Money came in, but it was not until 1994 that a narrowboat was bought from local resident Alex Gosling. Ruth Ray, a member of the committee, lives with her husband Colin in The Grove, which borders the canal, and a suitable mooring was found nearby. Colin, an engineer by profession, agreed to adapt the boat for its new purpose. There would be access for wheelchairs and a lift would also be installed to carry passengers down to the saloon. The boat was appropriately named *Maggie G*, after Margaret Gammon.

It can take a maximum of twelve passengers, and, since its first trip in 1994, it has become a familiar sight on the canal during the summer months. Trips are arranged to suit groups who have special needs and they last around an hour, travelling the

Maggie G.
(Photo provided
by Colin and
Ruth Ray)

3-mile Woking stretch of the canal. They start from either the Town Quay or from Arthur's Bridge and passengers may see a variety of wildlife including swans, herons and cormorants. On one occasion an enormous white puffball was sighted; another time a snake could be seen swimming in the canal.

There is no fee, but donations are welcome. The *Maggie G* provides an excellent service and deserves the support of the local community.

Marie Carlile House

The Church Army was founded in 1882 by Wilson Carlile. He lived with his sister Marie in Coley Avenue, Woking. In the 1950s he decided to use his house as a care home for the elderly. He named it Marie Carlile House after his sister. It functioned very successfully for many years. In 1974 Captain Jim Etheridge and his wife Margaret took over the running of it.

Sadly, at the beginning of the twenty-first century the Church Army decided to close the home and relocate the remaining residents. They were not happy, and neither was the community. The Church Army headquarters was bombarded with irate letters, which were ignored. In December 2000 many people attended the farewell service in the small chapel. It was led by Malcolm Herbert, the vicar of Christchurch.

The house was later demolished and flats were built on the site, though the name Marie Carlile still appears on the entrance.

Marie Carlile.

Maybury Centre.

Maybury Centre

The Central and Maybury Community Association was formed in 1987. Woking had become a multicultural town and a community centre where people of different backgrounds could meet was needed. A property was found in Board School Road and, as its name suggests, the building had originally been a board school in the nineteenth century. In the twentieth century it became Maybury Infant School; however, it was not until 1993 that work to convert the building into a community centre started.

The work was completed the following year. There was a large hall, two smaller halls, several rooms of varying sizes and a modern kitchen. Maybury Centre was officially opened by Sir Trevor MacDonald on 18 September 1994. Since then it has adapted to meet the needs of an ever-growing population.

Today it is a hive of activity, used by a variety of groups on a regular basis. Coffee mornings and social activities are held and there are activities for young people. It is used by operatic, drama and dance groups. No doubt it will continue to adapt and be used by Woking's multicultural society.

Market Place

Woking has had a market for many years. However, it changed its venue on a number of occasions. At one time it occupied the area near Victoria Arch. Then it moved to Commercial Way where stalls selling colourful dresses, scarves and children's clothes

Market Place.

stood beside others selling fruit, vegetables and exotic foods. Today, Market Place is situated in the covered way between Wolsey Place and The Peacocks. The clothes stalls have disappeared, but fruit and vegetables are still on sale. Also available are a selection of greeting cards, a cobbler and various fast foods.

(The) Martian Landing

In May 1895 H. G. Wells moved to Woking with his new wife; they lived in Lynton in Maybury Road. While there, he wrote his most famous book, *War of the Worlds*, which was published in 1898. In the novel, Martians invade the town of Woking and destroy it. The author and his wife left Woking soon after its publication and moved to Worcester Park. Perhaps he was embarrassed at having 'destroyed' the town!

In 1998, to celebrate the centenary of the book's publication, Michael Condron was commissioned to create a stainless-steel structure intitled *The Martian Landing*. It was an excellent representation of Wells' Martian. Standing 7 metres tall with legs set wide apart, its all-seeing eye peers down at the tiny residents who walk underneath it. On 8 April 1998 it was officially unveiled by television presenter Carol Vorderman.

The Martian.

Member of Parliament

Woking elected its first MP at the general election on Thursday 23 February 1950. A new Woking constituency had recently been formed. There were three candidates: Harold Watkinson, Conservative; Turner Bridges, Liberal; and Trevor Davis, Labour. Residents flocked to vote at designated polling stations. After these had closed, the sealed ballot boxes were taken to the police station and locked in the cells overnight.

Early the next morning they were taken to the Boy's Grammar School under police escort. Volunteers counted the votes all day. The result was announced at 5 p.m. by the returning officer, Captain Neville Lawrence, the High Sheriff of Surrey. Harold Watkinson, the Conservative candidate, won with a majority of over 11,000.

(St) Michael's Church, Sheerwater

After the Second World War many Londoners had lost their homes and needed new accommodation. The Sheerwater estate, near Woking, was one of the new neighbourhoods created to house the homeless Londoners. In the 1950s houses were built on woodland between the railway line and the Basingstoke Canal.

Three temporary buildings for Catholics, Anglicans and Methodists were erected, but by the middle of the 1960s all were in dire need of repair and were demolished. Catholics joined the worshippers at St Dunstan's Church near the railway station. One new Church, St Michael's, was built and it was dedicated on 24 April 1976. It was a daughter church of All Saints' Woodham and Methodists also used the building, as did the local community.

In June 2016, Revd Gillaine Holland was appointed as the new vicar and the church continues to be used by the congregation and the local community.

St Michael's
Church.

(St) Mary of Bethany Church

In the late nineteenth century the population around the Mount Hermon area was growing and a church was needed. Revd William Hamilton was the vicar of Christ Church – the town church. He was a wealthy man and wanted to use his money to benefit the town. In 1896 he bought two plots of land at the end of Mount Hermon Road. He left Woking in 1905 to move to Norfolk, but, as a parting gift, he gave money for the building of a church on the land he had bought. In 1906 the foundation stone of St Mary of Bethany was laid and building commenced. When it was completed, the church was consecrated as a chapel-of-ease to Christ Church.

The interior was light and airy because of the large windows, and it was brightly decorated. The wooden screen behind the altar was carved by Nathaniel Hitch, the famous sculptor. Choir stalls were installed on the north and south sides of the chancel. On the east wall of the church, the colourful stained-glass window was created by Heaton, Butler and Byrne.

St Mary of Bethany was one of the first buildings in Woking to have electricity. This was installed in 1907 and the church continued to grow. In 1923 the diocese of Winchester decreed that St Mary of Bethany should become a parish in its own right. It was not until 1927 that the diocese of Guildford was created.

The church's benefactor, William Hamilton, was not forgotten. In 1960, a hall dedicated to him was built on the south side of the church. The porch was demolished in 1974 and Hamilton Hall was linked to the main entrance on the west side by a new extension. In 1984 St Mary of Bethany became a Grade II listed building.

The late twentieth century saw a major redesign of the building. Anglican churches in the west always faced the east, towards Jerusalem, but St Mary of Bethany

St Mary of
Bethany.

broke with tradition. A dais was erected below the north wall and the seating was
rearranged so that the congregation faced the north instead of the east. Despite this,
the congregation continued to grow; regular services are held on Sundays and during
the week other activities cater for all sections of the community.

(St) Mary the Virgin Church

In the twelfth century it is likely that a stone chapel was built on the site of St Mary
the Virgin Church in Horsell. The present church, now a Grade II listed building, was
built in the fourteenth century although part of the west wall may be from an earlier
period. The west door still boasts the original hinges, latches and ironwork. The south
aisle was added in the fifteenth century.

There was more building during the next few centuries. The chancel was rebuilt in brick in the eighteenth century. The mediaeval screen was removed in the nineteenth century when the south aisle was extended eastwards. There were more changes in the twentieth century. The north aisle and the Trinity Chapel were added. Then, in 1987 a large room adjoining the church was built to accommodate the growing congregation.

Reminders of the past remain inside the church. There is a sixteenth-century iron spit, probably used to roast an ox or pig on special festivals. The oak chest in the porch dates from the sixteenth century while inside is another one dating from the previous century. An oak pulpit was installed in 1662. The baptistry was added in 1921 and the remains of two stained-glass windows dating from the fourteenth and fifteenth centuries can still be seen.

The six bells, established in the eighteenth, still call the congregation to church every Sunday but also ring out to celebrate special occasions.

Monument Bridge

In the seventeenth century James I granted the manor of Woking to Sir Edward Zouche. He was a man who liked to make his mark – a physical one so that he would be remembered. On Monument Hill, near the canal, he erected a 6-foot tower that loomed over the area. Sadly, for him, it collapsed in the 1860s during a violent storm. It gave its name to Monument Road. In the late 1930s Monument Bridge, spanning the canal, was built. In the twenty-first century a huge office block was erected beside the canal, but this has recently been demolished and the site now awaits some redevelopment. Monument Road and Monument Bride still remain as reminders of Sir Edward Zouche.

Monument Bridge.

Newark Priory

In the twelfth century, Ruald d'Calna de Saudes and his wife Beatrice founded Newark Priory, near Pyrford. Dedicated to the Virgin Mary and the martyred Thomas Becket, it became an Augustinian priory. The building was originally cruciform with cloisters, a kitchen and a farm; the tower and the gatehouse were separate. The monks would sometimes have worshipped at St Peter's Church.

In 1538 the priory fell prey to Henry VIII's Dissolution of the Monasteries. Today the south transept, part of the south wall and a section of the chapel are all that remain. The ruins, set in a field owned by a local farmer, can only be viewed from a distance.

Newark Priory.

On 14 June 1967 this Scheduled Ancient Monument became a Grade I listed building. A 'Sunrise Service', held beside the ruins every Easter Sunday, is led by the vicar of the Church of the Good Shepherd in Pyrford.

(St) Nicholas Church

In 1762 the two parishes of Pyrford and Wisley were joined. They are both only a short distance from the town of Woking. The Domesday Book mentions a church at Pyrford, but the current church – St Nicholas – was built in the twelfth century on a hill near the village. No additions have been added over the centuries and it seats only around a hundred. Restoration work in the nineteenth century revealed some interesting medieval frescoes on one of the walls, and three original consecration crosses can also be seen.

Elizabeth I often visited Pyrford and attended services at St Nicholas. Legend says that she presented the church with a small chalice, which is now housed in the treasury at Guildford Cathedral. St Nicholas continues to hold regular services and also serves the local community.

St Nicholas Church.

O

Ockenden Venture

Joyce Pearce, a teacher at the Woking Girls' Grammar School, was very concerned about the many displaced people in Europe after the Second World War. Having visited refugee camps in West Germany, she brought five girls aged between twelve and fifteen back to England. She installed them in Ockenden, her house in White Rose Lane. They attended Greenfield School and an appeal was launched for funds to support more refugees.

With the help of colleagues, including Ruth Hicks, the headmistress of Greenfield School, Joyce Pearce set up the Ockenden Venture to aid refuges from war-torn Europe, 'providing for their maintenance, clothing, education, recreation, health and general welfare'.

The Ockenden Venture became a registered charity in February 1955. The year 1959 was World Refugee Year and the Venture expanded overseas, setting up schools in India, Sudan, Pakistan, Cambodia and Algeria. The Venture was registered as a 'War Charity' in February 1960 and, in the New Year's Honours' List, Joyce Pearce was awarded an OBE for her work.

The film star Ingrid Bergman, visited Ockenden in July 1965, describing it as 'a unique movement which sets out to give a home and education to young refugees of every race, colour and creed'. The following year she made an appeal for it on the television show *Be So Kind*.

With the advent of civil wars in the 1970s and 1980s, more refugees needed help and the Ockenden Venture was happy to provide this. Joyce Pearce died in 1985, but she left a lasting legacy. The name was changed to Ockenden International in 1999. Today it is a funding agency and its programmes are run by other agencies.

Old Woking

Old Woking was originally called Wochingas by the Saxons. A Saxon nobleman, Brordar, founded a minster in the area. By the eleventh century the manor of Wochingas had become the property of the king. The manor of Woking, as it was now

Old Woking.

called, appears in William the Conqueror's Domesday Book. As Woking was part of the royal forest of Windsor, the king and his successors often hunted in the area.

When, in 1189, Richard I granted the manor of Woking to Sir Alan Basset, he probably built a manor house in the centre of the deer park. Surrounded by a moat, it would have been approached by a drawbridge, and the king and his retinue would have stayed there while hunting. In 1452 the manor reverted again to the Crown. A charter, giving permission for an annual fair to be held on the Tuesday after Whit Sunday was granted to the village. This, later to be known as the Toy Fair, continued to be held until the 1870s.

In the twentieth century the charter fair was revived by the Old Woking Village Association and held annually during the May bank holiday in the grounds of the White Hart Inn in the High Street. Sadly, the fair is now no longer held, as the White Hart Inn has disappeared.

Oriental Institute

In June 1860 Prince Albert laid the foundation stone near the railway line of the Royal Dramatic College. This was intended for 'decaying [retired] actors and actresses'. The building was completed two years later. In 1862 the first residents moved in and the college was officially opened in 1865. Unfortunately, it was not a success. In 1883 the money ran out and it had to be closed.

The same year the defunct building was bought by Dr Gottlib William Leitner. Asian students came to study and in 1889 a mosque was built in the grounds where they could worship. Renamed the Oriental Institute, this gave its name to Oriental Road. Unfortunately, Dr Leitner died in 1899 and, as there was no one to carry on his work, the institute and the mosque were closed. The site was later taken over by the Martynside Aircraft Factory, who used it until the factory closed in 1926.

Oriental Road

Named after the Oriental Institute (see opposite), in the nineteenth century this was a muddy tree-lined track passing through heathland. By the 1960s the land had been cleared and building started. Today it is a busy thoroughfare with a bus route to the town. The bus stop is outside St Paul's Church. On the other side of the road is Lion House, the headquarters of the James Walker Group which at one time had used the Oriental Institute building. This was later demolished and the Lion Retail Park took over the site. Further up the road is the Shah Jahan Mosque, built by Dr Leitner for his Muslim students to worship within.

Oriental Road.

(The) Parachute Company

For some time the GQ Parachute Company had designed and produced parachutes in Guildford. In 1934 the factory was moved to Portugal Road and four years later a new two-storey factory was built on the site. During the Second World War the company was kept very busy providing parachutes for the RAF. After the war, the company continued to produce parachutes on the same site for many years. Then, in 1987, the company relocated to South Wales and a block of flats was built on the Portugal Road site.

Flats on site of Parachute Factory.

Parrington's Garage

Kevin Parrington finished his secondary education at Winston Churchill School in 1970. For the next five years he worked as a motor vehicle apprentice at Inkerman Barracks in Knaphill. While there, he acquired a City and Guilds National Certificate as a craftsman and full technician. He then spent a year in America working with Volkswagen cars in Minneopolis.

Retuning to England, he planned to start his own business and at first he used a lock-up in Knaphill. Then he was able to buy a builders' yard in Portugal Road. On 16 September 1985 the contracts were signed. The council granted Kevin permission to change the site from a builders' yard to a garage and Parrington's Garage was open for business.

Over the years the garage expanded. As well as servicing cars, they were bought and sold. More staff were appointed. With his excellent reputation for good service, professionalism and integrity, Kevin soon attracted clients from all over the country.

In 2019 the office was moved to more spacious quarters on the opposite side of the road where Parrington's Garage continues to serve its loyal customers.

The original Parrington's Garage.

Park School.

Park School

In September 1923 Miss Katherine Maris, a Cambridge graduate, took up her post as headmistress of the new Girls' Grammar School. As there was no money available to build a new school, the girls took up residence in four First World War army huts in Coley Avenue. While there were covered pathways, the sides were open to the elements. However, good use was made of the limited facilities: one of the huts became a multipurpose hall; at one end was a stage that could be used for plays and the daily assembly; wall bars on one side indicated that it was used as a gymnasium; and every day it also became a canteen.

During the Second World War an air-raid shelter was built. The school was growing and accommodation was becoming 'desperate'. The problem was solved by building more huts! It was not until 1953 that a new Girls' Grammar School was built on the corner of East Hill and the Old Woking Road. The huts in Coley Avenue were demolished and a new purpose-built building was erected to accommodate boys and girls with learning difficulties. The Park School was opened and continues to flourish as an excellent school, like its predecessor.

Party in the Park

For eight years Woking Borough Council has hosted a party in Woking Park on a Saturday at the beginning of July. During the day it attracts over 10,000 visitors. If the party coincides with the Wimbledon Championships, visitors can watch the tennis on a large screen. There is something for everyone, and each year new items are added to the programme. There is no charge and there is plenty for both adults and children to enjoy.

There are opportunities for local talent to be displayed, visitors can dance to live music and there are plenty of activities in which to engage. Skateboarding is popular and there is a mobile mini-ramp on which adventurers can kick turn or 'pop an ollie' with help from the professionals. A new addition in 2019 was 'slacklining' – a form of tightrope walking but on a suspended line of webbing.

There is street theatre and, on the main stage, audiences are entertained by live performances by big-name acts, including finalists from *Britain's Got Talent*. Other attractions include a Punch and Judy show and a whirling urban astronaut who floats 20 feet up above the crowd. At midday there is a parade around the park led by the Carnival Band. A food village provides a number of stalls with a wide choice of food and drink, including craft beers. No doubt there will be other delights added in future years. The 2019 party concluded with a free outdoor screening of *The Greatest Showman*.

Patisserie Valerie

In 1926 Belgian-born Madame Valerie opened her first patisserie in Frith Street, London. This was followed by many more throughout the country. Patisserie Valerie opened in Wolsey Place in Woking in September 2013, but sadly it closed in 2019. The window was once full of delicious, colourful pastries, while the menu detailed the delightful concoctions that could be enjoyed in the café with a cup of tea or taken home to be devoured later. Cakes could also be made for special occasions or ordered online.

However, Patisserie Valerie did not only serve patisseries. There was plenty more on offer during the day: Continental breakfasts, as well as the traditional full English were available, or a hungry customer could also enjoy an all-day breakfast and brunch. At lunchtime grilled snacks or a two- or three-course meal was served. At teatime a Madam Valerie cream tea was not to be missed. Patisserie Valerie is a sad loss to the town.

Patisserie Valerie.

(St) Paul's Church

As the population of Maybury was growing, a church was needed in the area. In 1884 the foundation stone of St Paul's Church was laid in Oriental Road. The consecration of the church took place a year later. It was a daughter church of Christ Church, but in 1959 it became a parish in its own right. Because it was surrounded by trees, it was at first known as the Church in the Trees.

In 1995 St Paul's Church celebrated its hundredth birthday. By the twenty-first century most of the trees had disappeared, but one yew tree remained beside the east wall of the church; after much debate, it was decided that it should be cut down to make room for a small car park. It was removed in 2008 and the wood was cut up. A member of the congregation fashioned two crosses from it. One was placed outside on the south wall of the church; the other stands inside the church beneath the east window.

When, in 2005, the church celebrated the fiftieth anniversary of becoming a parish in its own right, the congregation was delighted to welcome back Geoffrey Shaw, the first vicar, to take part in the service. The adjoining church hall became the community hall and continues to be used by both the congregation and the local community. A variety of activities for all ages are held throughout the week. In 2019, the Bishop of Guildford opened the new 'Welcome Area', which can be used for meetings. On the left-hand side, patio doors open on to a small garden with seats. This is very popular when the sun shines.

Above: St Paul's Church.

Left: Inside St Paul's Church.

Peacocks Centre.

Peacocks Shopping Centre

During the latter part of the twentieth century Woking was being redeveloped. In the 1980s much of the town centre was demolished to make room for change. The seven-storey Peacocks Shopping Centre and car park opened. The lower floor was the food hall, home to a variety of eating places ranging from pizzas to pastries. Above this, the middle and upper floors both contain shops, including Debenham's – Woking's only department store. The next floor contains a car park and the box office for the Ambassadors' Theatre Complex. Nearby is the Auberge restaurant where theatregoers can eat before watching a performance. The two remaining floors are car parks.

Pine Trees

Although only 25 miles from London, a green belt area surrounds the busy town of Woking. There is an abundance of wooded areas where walkers can relax and forget the stress of modern life. The woods contain a great number of ancient pine trees. A hot summer can occasionally cause a fire in the woods, and the smell of burning pine trees wafts over the town.

Legend says that it was Sir Edward Zouche who introduced pine trees into Woking in the seventeenth century. He was a resident of Woking and attended St Peter's Church.

Above left: St Peter's Church.

Above right: Pulpit in St Peter's.

(St) Peter's Church

It was probably in the eighth century that a wooden church was built on the site of the original minster, founded in AD 625 by the Saxon nobleman Brordar. When William the Conqueror acquired the manor of Woking in the eleventh century, he replaced the wooden building with a new stone church dedicated to St Peter. A number of Saxon motives, including an iron cross, are engraved on the huge oak door at the west end of the church. This is the only part of the original wooden church that remains. In the thirteenth century the south aisle was added.

When, in the seventeenth century, Sir Edward Zouche acquired the manor of Woking, he built a gallery at the west end of the church to hold more parishioners. He also enlarged the pulpit, producing a three-deck, hooded version. In 28 August 1627, Charles I, who was visiting Woking, worshipped at St Peter's and heard a three-hour-long sermon.

In 1918 the lower sections of the pulpit were removed; the top section forms the present pulpit. The church today has a flourishing congregation and a variety of activities catering for all ages are held during the week. Opposite the church is a hall that sits beside the small car park.

Police Station

In the early twentieth century there were a few schools for young children run by the churches, but there was no secondary education. In 1910 land was bought in Guildford Road on which to build a secondary school for boys. It took four years to build, and in

Above left: Police station.

Above right: Cupola on the police station.

September 1914 the Boys' Secondary School opened with fifty boys. The school grew and by 1932 there were 331 boys on the roll.

In 1949 the name was changed to the Boys' Grammar School. The school continued to flourish and gained a reputation of its excellent plays, which were produced every year. However, the wind of change was blowing through the country and grammar schools were closing. One of these was the Boys' Grammar School in Woking, which closed in 1982.

The building, with its distinctive cupola, was eventually taken over by the police. It was adapted and another building was erected nearby to house the magistrates' court. The new police station and court complex was opened by the Duke of Gloucester on 18 October 1990. The police continued to use the site for many years, but they expect to move elsewhere soon.

Pool in the Park

The twentieth century saw an increase in leisure activities and in 1910 a primitive swimming pool was opened near the Hoe Stream, which supplied the water. The site was not ideal as it was near a refuse dump. It was not until 1935 that a new open-air swimming pool, built in the fashionable lido style, was opened in Kingfield Road and the original pool was closed. The new pool served the residents of Woking for many years, but in the twenty-first century it was replaced by a modern pool enclosed in glass. Residents could now swim in comfort in a warm atmosphere. To find a name for the new pool, a competition was held. A local primary schoolgirl won it with the appropriate, alliterative name Pool in the Park.

Pool in the Park.

Poppins Restaurant

Poppins Restaurant in Commercial Way provides a variety of meals throughout the day. A delicious breakfast of bacon and eggs, served on crispy fried bread can be enjoyed from 7.30 a.m. Tomatoes, mushrooms, baked beans and hash browns can be added to make a larger breakfast. Coffee, tea or a cold drink complement the meal. For lunch, visitors can choose from salads, burgers, jacket potatoes, omelettes, fish and chicken. A children's menu is also available. A selection of sweet dishes are available for dessert or afternoon tea before the restaurant closes 5.30 p.m.

Quakers

It was George Fox who, in the seventeenth century, founded the movement known today as the Quakers. He objected to the very formal pattern of worship used by the Established Church and decided to introduce a more informal type of worship. The movement proved popular, and, by the time he died in 1691, he had more than 50,000 followers.

There has been a Quaker meeting in Woking for many years. Worshippers meet in a house in Park Road. The meetings are informal and visitors are always welcome. The meeting room has access for wheelchairs and there is a small car cark. There are regular meetings on Sunday mornings when cars can also park for free in the road. On the fourth Sunday of the month a session is also held for children.

Monday evenings are used for other meetings. On the second Monday, members read from their book of faith and share ideas; the fourth Monday is used for contemplation and meditation and there is also a meeting entitled Becoming Friends, at which all are welcome to learn more about the Quaker faith.

Raistrick, George

George Raistrick, a wealthy landowner, was regarded by some as a great conversationalist, but by others as an eccentric. In the late nineteenth century, he lived on the southern side of the railway line. The main entrance to Woking station was on this side, and it was on this land that the local council intended to develop. Shops and houses were planned.

However, there was a major problem. George Raistrick owned much of the land and he refused to sell it for redevelopment. The council had to rethink its plans. Building started instead on the north side of the railway line. It was not until the twenty-first century that the main station entrance was established on the north side.

Raistrick was married and had two daughters and a son. In 1905 he became ill and died on 12 April that year. His simple coffin, bearing only the words 'George Raistrick died 12 April 1905', was taken by road to Guildford and then by train to Brighton. It was here, in the Raistrick family vault, that George Raistrick was laid to rest in the Extra Mural Cemetery in Brighton after a funeral service conducted by one of the chaplains.

Railways

In 1834 Parliament passed an Act authorising the building of a railway from London to Southampton. Individuals and companies from all over the country contributed money to pay for the project and work started on the new railway on 6 October 1834.

The Basingstoke Canal was used to ferry materials for the building of the railway. The first part of the line from Nine Elms – now Vauxhall – to Woking Common was completed in 1838. On Saturday 12 May of that year, a number of guests boarded the train at Nine Elms and travelled in style to Woking Common. Here, they were treated to a luxurious lunch in a nearby tent before boarding the train for their return journey.

There was another journey on the following Saturday. Two trains carrying 400 passengers travelled the same journey. Crowds along the route cheered as the trains passed by. At Woking Common more tents had been erected, and once again the passengers were entertained to lunch.

Station on the Oriental Road side.

The railway was now available to the public and, during the following week, over 1,000 passengers made use of the new form of transport. Woking railway station was a two-storey building on the Oriental Road side of the railway line, and the two platforms were connected by a footbridge. The station contained a booking office, a waiting room and toilets. There was also a stable block for horses, which were used for shunting the carriages. The large bell on the roof of the building was rung for five minutes before each train left. By 1840 the line to Southampton had been completed.

During the twentieth century the station building was renovated and the top storey removed. It was intended that the town would develop on the south side of the town, containing the main entrance to the station; however, the landowner refused to sell his land for development, so Woking developed on the other side of the railway line. It was not until the twenty-first century that the main entrance to the station was changed to the town side.

Reed, Karen

Karen Reed's murder in April 1994 was, without doubt, a case of mistaken identity. At the time her sister, Alison Ponting, was staying with her in Woking. Alison worked for the BBC World Service and in 1988 she married a Russian art dealer and they came to live in England. However, her husband had deceived her. It is likely that he worked instead for the Russian KGB. In March 1993 British police arrested him for two murders – apparently ordered by his bosses. He was given two life sentences, so Alison was virtually a widow.

She went to stay in Woking with her sister Karen. The police considered that, because of her connections, she was in danger and security equipment and panic alarms were installed in Karen's house. Both women were warned not to open the door to strangers. One evening they ordered a pizza and, when the doorbell rang, Karen assumed it was the delivery man. It was not. As soon as she opened the door, six bullets were fired at her and she fell, dying.

There is no doubt that it was the distraught Alison who was the intended victim. At her sister's funeral she wore a thick black veil to hide her identity, aware that security was tight, and plain clothes police were near her all the time. The murderer was never brought to justice.

Robinson's

In 1934, Alfred Wyles' drapery shop in Chertsey Road was bought by William Robinson. His store, named Robinson's, remained as a draper's but was also a women's outfitters. The latter became very popular. Elderly ladies would be driven to the shop and wait

Site of Robinson's.

while their chauffeur would summon a sales assistant. He would then go for a walk while she climbed into the car to measure the occupant for her corset.

When William Robinson retired, his son David and daughter Isabel continued to run the store, which also boasted an excellent restaurant on the upper floor. Sadly, the shop eventually closed and the site is now occupied by an estate agent.

Rhoda Mcgaw Theatre

The Rhoda McGaw Theatre has seating for 228. It was named after a Woking councillor and is situated at the bottom of the Ambassador's Complex, though it predates this. When the Ambassador's was erected in the 1990s, there were fears that the Rhoda McGaw would disappear. However, the local community sprang into action and bombarded the council with angry letters. The little theatre was so popular that it was allowed to remain. While owned by Woking Borough Council, it is managed by the Ambassador's, and tickets for the small theatre can be bought at the main box office.

The little theatre continues to be used by many local amateur groups. Some members of these, however, have professional qualifications. The theatre provides a variety of entertainment: plays, dance, opera and youth performances, and it also hosts the annual Drama Festival run by the Woking Drama Association. The theatre is busy throughout the year.

Salvation Army

The Salvation Army was established in Woking in the nineteenth century. The first 'soldier' – a sister – was enrolled in 1987. More brothers and sisters followed. and meetings were held regularly in local halls and in the open air. A permanent base was soon needed. Building started on an empty site on the corner of Church Street and Clarence Avenue. In 1897 the new Salvation Army hall was officially opened.

This continued in use until the 1970s when the area was redeveloped and the building had to be demolished. Eventually a new hall was built in Walton Road. On 15 April 1972 the Salvation Army Corps, with its famous band, marched through Woking to the new building for its official opening. Sadly, in 2005 there was yet more local development and once again the hall was demolished; later a block of flats was built on the site.

The Salvation Army's next home was in Sythwood, Horsell. The new building embraced modern technology, having a rainwater-harvesting plant, a ventilation

Salvation Army.

system and solar panels. Built for use by the community as well as the Salvation Army, it boasts a large worship area, a number of rooms and a café. Officially opened on 19 January 2008, it continues to be in constant use.

Sands

In the late nineteenth century, an inn was built on Horsell Common. Because the land around it was very desolate and bleak, Bleak House was considered an appropriate name. It was in no way connected with Chares Dickens' book of the same name! With the advent of the motor car, traffic increased and a main road was eventually constructed between Woking and Chertsey. Named Chertsey Road, it was soon a busy highway. As the road passed Bleak House, this provided a welcome break for those drivers who had already travelled some distance.

When the M25 was built in the middle of the twentieth century, Bleak House became even more popular for travellers heading for the motorway. In 2004 the brewery who owned the inn sold it. The new landlords felt the name Bleak House was rather depressing, so they changed it to Sands – a reminder of the sandpits on Horsell Common. The inn was adapted to provide accommodation with several en-suite rooms. There was also a luxury suite and free Wi-Fi. A Continental breakfast was provided for guests who stayed the night. The restaurant and bar provide a variety of dishes and drinks, and the traditional Sunday roast is also available. A garden behind the building can be used by visitors when the weather is suitable.

Sands.

Shah Jahan Mosque

In 1889 an Austrian professor, Dr Gottlieb Wilhelm Leitner, wanted to create an institute in England. Woking, with its new railway line, was an ideal place for it. The Royal Dramatic College, which had opened earlier, was now an empty shell. Dr Leitner transformed it into his Oriental Institute, which gave the road its new name of Oriental Road. He decided to build the first mosque in England nearby to cater for his Muslim students.

Influential Indian Muslims contributed money, including the ruler of Bhupal State, the Begum Shah Jahan. On top of the blue and gold dome was a gilt crescent and traditional minarets surrounded the walls. The mosque opened in 1889 and was named after its benefactor, Shah Jahan.

Sadly, Dr Leitner died ten years later, and the mosque was closed for several years. In 1912 a Muslim missionary, Khwaga Kasral Ud Dion, discovered the 'dirty neglected building' and resurrected it. It has been in use ever since, and other buildings to cater for more worshippers were erected in the grounds.

In 1948, after the partition of India, a number of Pakistanis came to England. Many settled in Maybury because of the mosque. Every Friday, crowds of worshippers flock to the Shah Jahan Mosque for prayers.

The Shah Jahan Mosque.

Shaw Centre.

(The) Shaw Centre

St Michael's School was founded as a small private school for boys in the 1930s. It was situated beside Wheatsheaf Common on Chobham Road. When it needed larger premises in the 1940s, the school was relocated to Brynford, a large house on the corner of Grange Road and Woodham Road. By now there were a few female pupils. Many of the boys took the Common Entrance examination and went on to public school at the age of thirteen. Some of the pupils attended the local grammar schools.

The school continued to flourish, but closed when the headmistress retired. St Michael's School merged with Hoe Bridge School on the Old Woking Road. Brynford was demolished and more houses were built on the site. The small road that was created to serve the new houses still bears the name Brynford Close.

The original building in Chobham remains. At one time it was a children's nursery, but then it was taken over by social services. Adapted as a 'Contact Centre', it took the name The Shaw Centre. Parents and grandparents can enjoy quality time with the children under supervision. Each room is named after a colour, and toys and books are available. There is also a table tennis table. The spacious garden contains various pieces of equipment for the children to enjoy, and nearby is a small car park.

Sheerwater

In the nineteenth century the area that is now Sheerwater was a natural lake. It was at the beginning of the twentieth century that the lake was drained by Lord King of Ockham, and the land was available for new housing. After the Second World War the area became one of the 'neighbourhood schemes'. These were estates where new houses could be built to house the many Londoners who had been bombed out of their homes. The area was named Sheerwater in remembrance of the lake that had once been there. It means 'clear water'. Houses, shops and three temporary churches were built. The temporary church buildings were demolished in the 1960s and a new church, St Michael's, was built to be used by the Methodists as well as the Anglicans. The Roman Catholic worshippers moved to St Dunstan's Church in Shaftesbury Road. In 2019 plans were made for the redevelopment of Sheerwater.

Smyth, Ethel

Ethel Smyth was born on 23 April 1858 in Sidcup, Kent. She studied music and became a prolific composer; she wrote songs, piano music, orchestral and choral works and operas. She moved to Hookheath in Woking at the beginning of the twentieth century and lived there for the rest of her life.

She was not only a musician, she also rode horses, played tennis and was a member of the ladies' section of the Woking Golf Club. In 1910 she joined the Women's Social and Political Union and became an enthusiastic suffragette. The following year she wrote 'The March of the Women', which became the anthem of the Suffrage Movement. She was imprisoned for throwing a brick through a politician's window. While there, the suffragette prisoners marched in the quadrangle singing their anthem; Ethel conducted them out of the window with a toothbrush.

Sadly, she started to lose her hearing and eventually became totally deaf. Unable to compose, she turned to writing and wrote ten books based on her own life. In 1922 she was made Dame Commander of the Order of the British Empire. In 1928, to celebrate her fifty years as a composer, a concert was held in the Boys' Grammar School and the composer herself conducted.

She died in 1944 at her home in Hookheath at the age of eighty-six. Her brother, Bob, a brigadier in the British Army, scattered her ashes near the Woking Golf Club where she had often played. She was not forgotten. The American premier of her opera *The Wreckers* was performed in New York in September 2007 by the American Symphony Orchestra.

(The) Sovereigns

Because of the increased traffic caused by the new railway, a railway hotel was built in 1840 in Guildford Road on the north side of the station. This catered for the mail coaches that now trundled through Woking; stables were also provided for the horses. Inside the cosy bar, passengers could relax with a drink while the horses could drink from the trough on the green outside.

The Sovereigns.

As the population increased, the town grew and houses were built to accommodate the growing number of commuters. The hotel was no longer necessary, so the building was enlarged and renovated. It continued to serve as an inn, and over the years it changed hands several times.

Today it is owned by the Ember Group and known as The Sovereigns. It no longer provides accommodation, but visitors can still enjoy a variety of drinks and choose from an extensive menu. Sunday lunch is very popular, as it has a selection of delicious roasts.

Spy at the Garage

In 1942 Methold's garage in Ripley, near Woking, reorganised its motoring business to help the war effort. It changed its name to Methold Engineering Ltd and started to produce parts for aircraft. Two skilled male machinists and around sixteen women comprised the workforce. As most of the women were foreign, they had to be carefully screened by the Labour Exchange before being accepted for work at Methold's.

Unfortunately, one of them slipped through the security net. During a night shift she loudly scoffed at the preposterous idea that there were concentration camps in Germany. A fellow worker hotly disputed this. To prove her point, she displayed the brand on her arm which had been put there during her time in one of those camps. When her antagonist refused to believe her, she flew at her and a vicious fight ensued.

The two women were eventually separated and held until the police arrived. They were taken to the police station. Neither of the women arrived for work the next day, but a policeman explained that while the concentration camp victim would return to work, her assailant would not. She would be 'detained during His Majesty's Pleasure'. Methold's Engineering had, unknowingly, been harbouring a spy!

Surrey History Centre

Goldsworth Road had been the home of Goldsworth Primary School for many years. As the number of pupils increased, more rooms were needed. Eventually, a purpose-built school was erected in Bridge Barn Lane, near the canal. It is still in use, though the original building was demolished.

For many years, Surrey, with its fascinating history, had needed somewhere in which to house its vast archives. The empty site vacated by the school was ideal. An impressive new building was erected and given the name of the Surrey History Centre. Material was collected from around the county.

Today the centre houses a wealth of material that illustrates Surrey's history – from the twelfth century to the twenty-first. There are 6 miles of records in the strongroom. Elsewhere, there are ancient documents, maps, photographs, newspapers, magazines and other memorabilia. Some documents are on micro-file.

To the right of the reception area is a large room resembling a library. The bookshelves contain a collection of both ancient and modern books. The centre of the room is occupied by tables, upon which are book rests. To use the facilities, visitors must possess a local library card. All bags must be left in the lockers and only a pencil and a notebook may be taken in. For research purposes, assistants are available to 'order' the books or documents that are required.

Foyer at Surrey History Centre.

T

Tante Marie

In 2015 the Tante Marie restaurant opened in Commercial Way. Sadly, this is no longer open, and the Academy itself ran into financial problems in 2018 and has also now closed. The Academy, the oldest independent cookery school in the United Kingdom, was first established in Woking in 1954 by Iris Synell, a local cookery writer. When she died in 1964 it continued to function under new management in Woodham House, Carlton Road. In the twenty-first century it relocated to Alexander House in Commercial Way.

Tante Marie.

The Academy trained students in cordon bleu cookery and hospitality management. The students were awarded diplomas and could gain experience by serving as waiters and waitresses in the restaurant. Many of them left the Academy to pursue successful careers elsewhere in catering and hospitality. Gap-year students could also take advantage of courses, which counted towards the Duke of Edinburgh Award. Many then obtained holiday jobs in hotels.

When the restaurant was open there was a small teaching kitchen, Tante Marie Live, at one end. Here, a maximum of eight students of all abilities were offered a wide variety of courses. These were run during the day, in evenings and at weekends. There were also men-only classes and ones for children. It is unfortunate that this excellent Academy no longer functions.

Trinity Methodist Church

The Methodists had first worshipped in Woking in 1863. They had had several venues over the years, but by the middle of the twentieth century the congregation had grown, so a permanent base was needed. In the late 1850s Alwyne House, on the corner of Brewery Road and Chobham Road, had been built by the Spencer Chapman family, who lived in it until 1927 when it was sold to another family. Until the 1960s it continued as a family home, but during this decade it was demolished.

The site remained empty for a while, but then the Methodists raised enough money to purchase it and the building of a new church commenced. When it was completed, Trinity Methodist Church became an impressive local landmark. The worship area is large and light while the surrounding rooms are used both by the congregation and the local community during the week.

The church also boasts a kitchen and an area for refreshments. It has a flourishing congregation and today it is often a hub of activity.

Below left: Flats named Alwyne Court.

Below right: Trinity Methodist Church.

Unwin's Printing Works

Unwin's Printing Works was founded by Jacob Unwin in the nineteenth century. When a fire destroyed the original buildings, he looked for a new site. In Old Woking he discovered a derelict watermill dating from Saxon times, which had been recorded in the Domesday Book. In 1869 new buildings were built on the site and it became Unwin's Printing Works. Later, the name was changed to the Gresham Press and it flourished until the twenty-first century when it became part of Martin's Printing Group.

Today the printing works is no more, and the buildings have been adapted to create a number of luxurious flats. This block of flats has the name Gresham Mill – a link with both the printing works and the ancient watermill.

Gresham Mill.

Victoria

In the year 1897 Queen Victoria had her Diamond Jubilee. During that year the foundation stone of a new hospital was laid near the Wheatsheaf Bridge. The new hospital was named the Victoria Cottage Hospital in honour of the queen. It was extended in 1903 and continued to serve the residents of Woking until 1990. That year

Victoria Arch.

Woking Community Hospital opened in Heathside Road. The Cottage Hospital was demolished and apartment blocks now stand on the site.

In 1901 Queen Victoria died. Th twentieth century continued with her son Edward VII on the throne. His mother left an indelible mark on the country, so it was not surprising that her name, 'Victoria', was not forgotten. At the western end of the town the Railway Arch was renamed Victoria Arch. The High Street, running beside the railway line, contained a number of shops. At the end of these and east of Victoria Arch a small park was established in 1904, named Victoria Gardens.

Victoria Gardens (Sparrow Park)

The small park at the end of the High Street was named Victoria Gardens after the late queen. It attracted a number of sparrows, which flocked there on a regular basis. Because of this, the name was later changed to Sparrow Park; however, it was soon taken over by the pigeons. Sparrow Park has now disappeared, but the pigeons are still in residence on the site.

Sparrow Park.

War Memorial

During the 1920s it was decided to erect war memorials throughout the country to commemorate those who had fallen during the First World War. Woking erected its war memorial in 1922 in Woking Park, at the south end of the town.

It was later moved to Sparrow Park near the Victoria Arch where it remained for over fifty years. After the Second World War many more names were added to it. In 1975 the memorial was thoroughly cleaned and moved to the town centre. Draped in the Union flag, it was ceremonially hoisted in its final resting place in the

War memorial.

Town Square near Christ Church. On 11 May 1975 a huge crowd gathered to watch the Lord Lieutenant of Surrey unveil it. The vicar of Christ Church then led a short service of remembrance. A service of remembrance is held in the same place every Remembrance Day.

Wells, H. G.

In May 1885, H. G. Wells moved to Woking with his mistress, Anne Catherine Robbins, known as 'Jane'. He married her in October 1885, and they lived in Lynton, Maybury Road, until 1898. His first science-fiction novel, *The Time Machine*, was published soon after they arrived. During his time in Woking, Wells wrote a number of books, and by the time he left he felt his writing career was 'fairly launched at last'.

In his most famous book, *The War of the Worlds*, Martians invade the town of Woking and destroy it. The book was published in 1898 and, soon after its publication, the novelist and his wife moved to Worcester Park. Perhaps he was worried that Woking residents might not react kindly to his novel. By now, his fame had spread across the world and many clamoured to meet him. After his wife, Jane, died in 1927, Wells returned to London. He died at the age of seventy-nine in Regent's Park on 13 April 1946.

Below left: H. G. Wells statue.

Below right: H. G. Wells Centre.

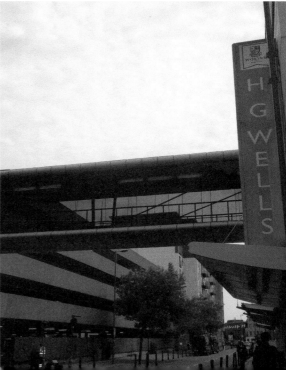

Woking's famous son was not forgotten by the town. In 1994 a community play, *Running Red*, was performed in his honour. The year 1998 was the centenary of the publication of *The War of the Worlds*. To celebrate this, the H. G. Wells Centre was opened in Commercial Road. This is still a popular venue for meetings and dinners, and is used by a variety of groups.

Erected nearby was a 7-foot stainless-steel statue – *The Martian Landing*. The sculptor was Michael Condron and his work is an accurate representation of Wells' Martian. Its legs are set wide apart and on its head a visor represents an all-seeing 'eye'. The structure was unveiled on 8 April 1998 by television presenter Carol Vordorman. Later, a statue of H. G. Wells was erected outside the Lightbox. This was later moved and is now part of a heritage walk.

Woking Homes

In the late nineteenth century, Revd Canon Allen Edwards of All Saints' Church in Lambeth was the railway chaplain. He was concerned about the number of homeless 'railway orphans'. He bought a house in Jeffreys Road in Clapham and in 1886 a number

Woking Homes.

of 'fatherless girls' moved in. Railway workers donated money for its upkeep. Canon Edwards set up the London Orphanage and South Western Servants' Orphanage as a charity with a board of governors. Before long, the number of girls reached fifty and another house was bought to cater of the growing numbers. In 1895 a third house was bought for 'fatherless boys'.

Canon Edwards was worried that the smoky London air was not healthy for the children, so he looked elsewhere for accommodation. In 1907 the charity purchased several acres of land in Oriental Road and the foundation stone was laid for a new orphanage. The building was completed in 1909 and 150 orphans moved in. Boys and girls were in separate units. They went to local schools and on Sundays they attended the church service at nearby St Paul's Church. The name was changed in the 1920s to the Southern Railwaymen's Home for Children. After leaving school, the girls usually went into service while the boys worked on the railway.

By the middle of the twentieth century the number of orphans had declined; the last one left the orphanage in 1989. The buildings were then adapted to home senior citizens and the name was changed to Woking Homes. There was a commemorative service in St Paul's in 1985 to celebrate the founding of the original orphanage.

In the 1990s a conservatory was added on to the lounge and a heated indoor swimming pool was built. These latest additions were officially opened in August 2000 by the railway artist David Shepherd. Building work continued into the twenty-first century. Every year in July Woking Homes hosts a garden party in its grounds, and this is always well supported by the local community and relatives of the residents.

Woking Palace

In 1189 Sir Alan Basset was granted the manor of Woking by Richard I. The 40-acre deer park had been a popular hunting ground for successive kings, so Sir Alan built a manor house in the middle of the park. Here, he could entertain royalty. A moat surrounded the building and there was a drawbridge for entrance, and a stable area was added later.

The complex expanded over the years, and by the fourteenth century an extra hall and two large chambers accommodated the royal visitors. Over the years the manor of Woking changed hands several times. In 1466 it was in the possession of Lady Margaret Beaufort, the mother of Henry VII. The king frequently stayed in the manor house. In 1503 he instigated changes to the house and transformed it into a luxurious royal palace. His son, Henry VIII, continued the work and enlarged it.

Unfortunately, Henry's successors rarely visited, and the buildings were not maintained. In 1620 Sir Edward Zouche was granted the manor of Woking by James I. He was not interested in repairing the palace and gradually it fell into disrepair. Zouche even used some of the bricks from the decaying walls to build himself an impressive new manor house nearby.

Above: Model of Woking Palace in the Lightbox.

Below: Ruin of Woking Palace.

Today the palace is a ruin. However, there have been several excavations that have turned up some interesting finds. On heritage days visitors are led by a guide around the ruined palace, which was once a building 'fit for a king'.

Wolsey Place

Thomas Wolsey was Archbishop of York and Henry VIII's Chancellor, so it is likely that the king would have invited him to visit Woking and to stay at Woking Palace. It is possible that Wolsey was at the palace in September 1515 when the news reached him that Pope Leo X had elevated him to the rank of cardinal. Later he upset Henry because he refused to agree to the king divorcing Catherine of Aragon so that he could marry Anne Boleyn. Wolsey set off from Yorkshire to travel to London to answer charges of high treason. He escaped his fate, however, as he died on 29 November 1530 of natural causes in an abbey in Leicester before he could reach London.

When Woking was redeveloped in the twentieth century Cardinal Wolsey was not forgotten, despite only having a slight link with the town. The covered shopping centre opposite Christ Church was named Wolsey Place.

Wolsey Place.

Woolworths and Wetherspoons

In 1926 the famous F. W. Woolworth store opened in Chertsey Road, Woking. During the Second World War, the Luftwaffe dropped a bomb in the area and part of the store was destroyed. It was not until 1958 that the original building was demolished, to be replaced by a more modern building. This building also disappeared during one of Woking's redevelopments. Woolworths closed and today the site is occupied by Wetherspoons, the popular bar and restaurant that serves a variety of food and drink all day long.

Wetherspoons.

Xylophone

At one stage in his life, Patrick Moore, the famous amateur astronomer, taught in St Andrew's School in Woking. As well as his obsession with *The Sky at Night*, he was also an accomplished musician. He bought a xylophone and taught himself to play. He soon became a very well-known, proficient player and he also wrote articles about the instrument. He often appeared on television with a xylophone instead of a telescope. In 1982 and 2013 he played in the band that was raising money for *Children in Need*. As well as playing, he also composed pieces and, in 2008, he played one of his own compositions on *Penguin Parade* on YouTube.

Sadly, he eventually had to give up playing because of his increasing arthritis. He died in 2012 and in 2015 his xylophone was sold at auction.

York Road Project

The York Road Project was officially formed in 2001 and registered with the Charity Commission. However, it had started years before when a number of volunteers from local churches in Woking walked the streets of the town offering soup and sandwiches to people who were sleeping rough. This developed into a 'Winter Watch' project supported by Shelter, and Woking Borough Council also became involved – some houses were made available in York Road for emergency accommodation between November and February. Eventually this embryo project became an official charity.

The York Road Project deals with men and women aged eighteen and over regardless of disability, race, religion or sexual orientation. While primarily serving the local community, queries from other parts of Surrey are considered. Woking Borough Council has leased furnished houses in York Road to the charity. These provide accommodation for single homeless people. As well as one main emergency property, there are four others catering for those who are able to 'move on'. Currently there is a total of twenty-nine beds, and the charity now functions throughout the year.

Z

Zizzi

Zizzi's restaurant in Goldsworth Road is one of several restaurants in Woking serving traditional Italian fare – pizzas, pasta, risotto – as well as dishes from other countries. Visitors can also sample a variety of both vegetarian and vegan dishes. It opens seven days a week, serving lunch and dinner. There is also a takeaway service. It is a popular eating place for the many Italians who have made their homes in Woking. Every year

Inside Zizzi's.

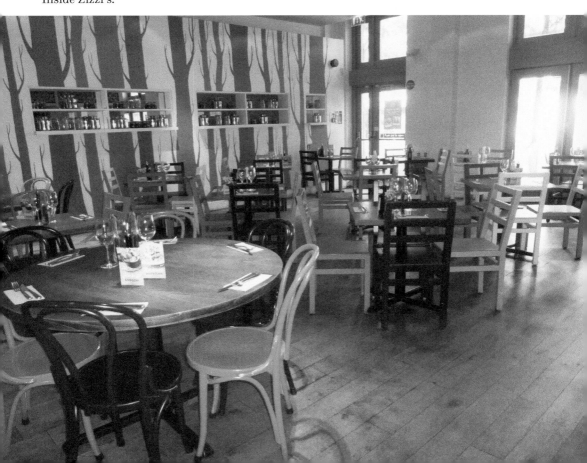

villagers from Italy visit Chobham Common to earn money by picking mushrooms. Many of them visit Zizzzi's during their stay.

Zouche, Sir Edward

In 1618, James I sold the manor of Woking to Sir Edward Zouche. The new owner continued for a while to entertain at the palace, but as no repairs had been carried out for many years, the building gradually fell into disrepair. Zouche was not interested in repairing it. Instead he demolished it and, using some of its bricks, built himself an impressive new mansion, Hoe Place, near the Hoe Stream, a tributary of the River Wey. Nearby, he also built a 60-foot octagonal tower, which sadly collapsed in a violent storm in 1869. Today, the only memory of it is the name Monument Road.

Sir Edward attended St Peter's Church and introduced some new features to the building. At the west end he erected a gallery and he installed a three-deck hooded pulpit. In 1918 the two lower decks of this were removed, but the top of the original structure was retained and continues to serve today as the pulpit.